Given

Given

poems

Arielle Greenberg

Verse Press
Amherst, MA

Published by Verse Press

Library of Congress Cataloging-in-Publication Data

Greenberg, Arielle.
  Given : poems / Arielle Greenberg.-- 1st ed.
    p. cm.
  ISBN 0-9723487-1-9 (pbk. : alk. paper)
  I. Title.
  PS3607.R448 G58 2002
  811'.54--dc21

                    2002013634

Book designed and composed by J. Johnson.
Text and display set in Mrs Eaves.
Cover art by D'vora Greenberg.

Printed in Canada
9 8 7 6 5 4 3 2 1

FIRST EDITION

CONTENTS

(caveshow)

2° Gaslight

given to Rob, a gift

"The keys to. Given! A way a lone a last a loved a long the"

James Joyce, *Finnegans Wake*

"Into a sweeping meticulously—
detailed disaster the violet
light pours. It's not a sky
it's a room…"

Frank O'Hara, "Joseph Cornell"

Afterwards, There Will Be a Hallway

The sky is violet like no other hypnosis.

Out the night window, the moon is a slip of coin over the skyscraperscape,
gold and red grids of night windows.

We (the clown, the doll, the murderer and I) are in love.
With the moon.

She ascends: the sky purples, clouds, she rises, now grinning,
becoming a burning door. We love her still.

So that when she begins the medusa eclipse,
we do not look away. We are sweetened.
We are sweetened out of sight.

The apocalypse afterwards is muddy and bound to our apartment.
Someone, one of us, takes advantage and is after. The rest of us collapse
in corners. Am I waiting for the soft thump or for administering it?
In the dark, our bodies are rag. We belong to the group. There is a limp,
and a dizzy.

Afterwards, there will be a hallway. I am anxious at both ends.

1° Waterfall

Soft Touch

He once got hit by a playground and it was all over for him with pockets. He couldn't eat breakfast for all the empty spaces. Holes distracted him. It was "as a child." But he wandered like a blank, sputtered, lost it.

When we married and I sat with him in a park or office, he would want to call me at home. "I want to call Cathy." And I would say, "But I am Cathy. I'm here. I'm your wife." And he'd say, swingset, "I know you are, but I want to call the *other* Cathy." And so later at home there'd be a recording of his voice on the machine: "I just wondered what you were doing right now."

The mind is a soft substance, a kind of pudding. Two million people have it, and it's caused by things we think are fun. By entertainment. Everyone has been touched by it in some way. Soft touch.

Was the other Cathy living in our house like a sock, like a closet, a shadow, a snake? Was I another Cathy? She became an oatmeal on my tongue, on his. Me. The other Cathy. The other wife. The one he'd call when I was right by him.

"Is the other Cathy like me?" I asked him. "Oh, no," he said. "You're a lot easier to talk to." And I felt a little bad for Cathy then. The other me. But I had been the one feeding him out of my enormous pockets. My big white blouse. The other Cathy was just the hole in his morning meal, a fruit you open.

People get impacted by a game or a junglegym or some other form of violence and when they wander away I see them. I guess they could be more angry, suddenly very sweet, or afraid of bridges. In love with a thing they never knew before. A slight shift is all it takes.

Tornado at the Dairy Queen

We were there as a reunion. It's no joke,
but an ice cream place in the middle of a nation
in the middle of an era near its ending like a fable
right in the middle of a tornado. All the frosty-freezes and swirl cones.
All the soft serve flurry metaphors intended, right.
Inside the exclamation mark, a fuzz of alumni
wrung the ankles of our new neighbors, kissed, wept,
and the thing that came at us came at us with its white and terrible roar.
It doesn't sound like thunder or a train going past.
They say it but no. Imagine sugar with all those chunks of chemicals
    inside
and whipped through a froth-maker. Imagine it. You can't imagine.
The alumni and counter workers and prom-night parents praying
and clutched, just a grip in the dark, in the walk-in,
six adults in a cooler in the middle of a nation
with almost no ears left, and certainly no roof. Barely
walls when we got out. A foot of wall
hardly. Just a mess—paper cups and brick,
that one sobbing girl, scoops, void of wind
where wind was. Thank you. We thought we would
die. We were still wearing the right kind of white hats.
In the midst of it, we saw nothing. The sweetness twisting furious past.

House of Precision

There are maybe three blocks between x and the House of Precision.
Loneliness hails x.
A loaf of stale bread for pudding x.

Winter is perhaps evident but doesn't want any poems written about it.
Hides in the lead village where Senator x fights the paper revolution.
All white.
Snowflakes more razor-cut than any love affair x ever knew.
All the people are x, and all the people are heaps of coal,
    and all the people are burning in their slivers.

The heaps of coal forgive someone else.

What goes on in the House of Precision?
Bricks made of glass. x communication.
A ballet of telephone wire disagrees:
It's a fortress, for "x offenders." Punk rock.
A ballad of shipping supplies says uh-uh,
    what we have here is naughty girls, very naughty.

Algebra, kisses in every squalid grid.
Boxes missing only o.

[untitled]

let's make out tonight in a certain interesting way
as the dogs switch their wallets from hand to hand in the yard
tonight will be very long with the pieces of flower vase still in the
      flooring
& there's a new rule about soap & about cardamom which doesn't
      run in your family
but we both know what we mean when we talk about the musical
      legacy of other people's cars
so here's an offer I'm wrapping up to you in edible flowers: let our
      mouths be particularly unusual & slow

with the dogs wet outside in the grass of tonight

You Need to Ease Up About Promises

I.   Witness

"So I took [the old man] by the shoulders, looked him square in
the eye, and said, sir, as God as my witness, I will save your house,
but you must get away from here right now."

D.L., firefighter, 8.30.00

So you'll save my house.
So what.
Will you save my shoulder or my playing cards?
Will you save my collapse?
Will you save my safety lock, safe deposit box, safe
keeping, failsafe, or all that has been dismantled?
You stop saving my house and I'll stop starting fires.
Said the phenomenon in the mystery. To the mystery.
Save it from what?
It is meant to be eaten by the unliquid, unsolid reds.
I have no witness.
I have no witness but I will shake you down.
My mortgage is all over the hayseed.

II.   I'm a Man Who Manufactures

What is that long, ugly, stupid, two-dollar shit you make?
I'm some sort of gopher or mole.
Cornflake Especially.
A Midwestern Conglomerate.
A puppet. A magnate.
I own a factory.
I make chairs.
I look a bit like Jimmy Carter, but it's the 70s, so it's easy to say that.
I'm a man who manufactures chairs. And everywheres.
There's a song about it.
I fight with community members (puppets) who are not productive:

the owl, the witch-lady, the king.

I may have fought with the king.

It's hard to be a post-industrial capitalist in a rather sloppy monarchy, everyone named after days in the week.

Besides, I'm indubitably Midwestern. Why *king*?

And is this a game show?

I may be modeled after Post or Kellogg.

Hey, is this a game show?

III.   Promises

The cat went up in the burning house of tight.

Legs went up, wicker went up, we told a story.

Your hair was redder. Mine.

A chair to lift. An owl—

the brush of blackness at its departure.

The house went up with two yellow eyes and its turned-around head.

The cat was making an American noise.

I said to you,_____.

I said to you, this is our wedding plan.

I have burned my dance card.

We danced on Ohio.

The children became gone.

The Expert

I eat salt when I am thirsty. Until my nose runs salt and then I cry. Until my lips go numb and then I drink a grain of something which dehydrates straight from the heart, the lung, an array of bluish organs.

I know thirst very well because I once belonged to that organization. It was a long time ago—I was in college and it was part-time, mostly mornings. Thirst loved me and recently, in fact, sent me a $250 check out of nowhere. Just for completing the census. Just for existing in a time of great pain. It's difficult to accept such a generous gift, but thirst is an affluent and guilty employer.

Thirst looks like a pool, an indoor swimming pool you install in the bathroom, a pool with a strong current. A lap-swimmer's pool for city dwellers. Thirst comes in the back of *The New York Times Magazine*.

I am lonely without other women poets who are hungry. In a crowd of women poets, eating, as often not eating, I am lonely. I eat from the bottom of the mines up, as if I can devour my way out, as if my throat is an open shaft, as if the white does not burn, as if the language has that fine sting, and I am working, a salaried Girl Friday to the salt.

Teaching English at a Two-Year College

I've been teaching English at a two-year college and it isn't going well.
Every single one of my students is somehow a furious dolphin.
We squeak at each other, the chalk squeaks
a little churchmouse runs into the one-room schoolhouse and
    throws up its arms and squeaks

the old-fashioned furnace squeaks

the sun in its dim winter tenement squeaks.
I can't help the suddenly spider monkey students to language
nor can I help myself: Language, a fat white lemon cake
cordoned off in the middle of the room, a bar of delicious soap.

Then what? Then I am running or then I am naked
or then I am faced with a battery of multiple-choice math tests.
I don't wake frozen or screaming. My bed is very cozy,
the sheets unwashed. The now back to being dolphin students learn
    the word "unwashed"
but don't need it, living as they do in the bathtub.

Your Mother, Who Can't Tell a Story

»　　　　The Flurry of Medicine

you are attached to a hum
(joined by a hum)
kidnapped by noiseless "healers"
& the palms of their sugary hands
oh believe it
this won't last
or the calm of theory
or the false waterfalls
which are about as movie-like
as concentric as
what can you say about the lack of anger here?
what can you, a practitioner of no good, say about silence?

»　　　　A Singular Building Appears in the Landscape

A novelist you know has never seen it before.
You are twins at a black-eyed carnival.
You are across the sea from the suburbs. You really care.
This is no good.
The architect is not making predictions now—
she is drawing blueprints across the table.
Moves her cat to one side.
This is no good.
Must find a way to bring people closer to the windows.
The novelist wears his ring from the voyage.
He says, *this is no longer the city in my dream.*

»   Your Mother, Who Can't Tell a Story

Has never used paint as much as paper.
Who will not have an animal of any kind.
At two o'clock, she took the minutes at the meeting.
At maybe four, she told someone off.
You wonder how you learned to eat with chopsticks at all.
Is her friend in or out of the class?
The edge of the narrative drifts menacingly near.
It isn't crafted for pedestrians.
She would make a bad movie.

»   When the Rain Feels like Softy

she says, & you remember the song
the chair that swiveled
her ungodly fear of giant squid
(which counter-indicated responsibility)
so you say, *crush your vision*
go on, it's fine today
this won't last
but it tastes of steel
of the castle rebuilt at the fairground
& you are still wearing the price of admission

A Proposal for a Longer Work
(Preferring the Dunes)

The project of the line editors choose the outtake loop

The project in which the white people don't speak like that

The project in which the forest trails *are* the roads

The project of atrophied limbs come into symphony

The project where you put QUE at the ends of people you never
    knew (strangers)

The project in which you question the desire for heroes

The project of opening her mouth from the inside

The project where you learn to write in boxes the proper noun
    "Kimberly" and the noun "lamb"

The project to attack in writing what you really want to write: little,
    pokey, cake

The project of recording the crossword of jargon

The project that loves to hang its head out the car window and
    smell the ocean

The project of you can make her mine

Lab

The cave I have is very small.
The cave in my throat is a cavity.
You can't fit the x-ray film inside without bending it.

My strand reminds a guy of a martini.
Inside my tissue, two men bicker.
Someone lights a torch, looking for a way out.

The day my mother got back from Florida.
And I carried the invisible alligators all around town, in the sky.
To move boxes of books or practice dancing.

The test will come back from the lab.
First there is a bucket of solution.
First there is a twist.

You don't want to hear any more about the Bay Area.
But let me tell you, this might be my last chance.
My teeth are also smaller than usual teeth.

Statistics are no surprise.
They are my father's business: punch cards.
You'll find out, or you won't, and someone will be distracted.

Pharmacodynamics

Where is the art in falling apart?
Do you coddle it from a glass mold like good pudding,
slowly, its jelly edge? (Tenterhooks. Eggshells. Soufflé.)
Where's your tin badge from the disaster?
How many pieces have been recovered—sixty-five, a hundred,
an ear next to an orchestra of intestines?
At night there are the shakes, red-brilliant, fists;
the morning sputters into a ghost town
where the apparition of nightmares *a carpet of inchworms,*
your father's death hang around porches like saloon girls
drunk on varnish, just idle horror.
You wake up and your bed is at sea.*
(all day) Leather repair, stop light, telephone,
you ache to swim back the long green mile to it
and drown, loved. You'd love to drown. You'll practice.
Famished. Pills. Trifles. The chemistry is off;
you are a fouled science fair project, blue where the pink
     should have been,
no air, no energy. Where is the powder for lifting these clouds?
Your teeth ask the questions while you sleep like telegraph,
sets your jaw in pain. The fingers don't answer,
the prescription, the stream of screaming,
toilet or some other white paper bounding off its tube down
     a flight of stairs.
There is no final grade—you as god, relentlessly,
no refills. Alone with the sawdust, you stop sweeping up.

---

* See: the sea, the house in the water, the bed in the house,
Fatty and Mabel Adrift in the bed, flipped by waves,
floating bed, doggy paddle, nothing dry?

Startle

They were only too proud to comply.

They were indigenous to the area, but ache had monopolized the small storefronts and hand-painted service shingles: the ache of hunger.

And so they hungrily prevailed, like a den of cats forced to build the pyramids.

They held their chins high.

They were free to be startled by their bondage.

It was a fresh addiction each new day, laboring this way, and their pale minds and hearts, rooted readily in the exchange of silver for oil, aluminum for silk.

When the guerrillas reached the gate of the ghetto, it swung open easily (it had never been locked), and they were weepily emancipated.

They left carrying the bricks in their teeth like newborn cubs.

The Alexander Technique

Joe DiMaggio has not told me any secrets for so long.
    God's lonely eye has not turned to tell me any secrets.
Freud developed psychoanalysis to cure his own talking of secrets
   out loud to me.
    Virginia Woolf's shawled Indian girl hasn't told me any secrets.
A problem.

The men touching the tops of their hair haven't told me any secrets.
    Enigma tells me no secrets (let me get the words all right).
The present indicative says nothing.
Do not say a thing.
    A different energy makes a move to tell me all its secrets, but retracts.
William Carlos Williams held patents, but none were patents on form,
   and the patents tell me
nothing.
    Slow trains bark a track but don't tell secrets.

On a little island off the little island of Sicily, secrets pile up under piles.
    The French say *non* in the act of love, but close the closet door.
Mum. As the grave.
    I don't want to tell you how you've hurt me, so I tell the teacher.

An Edwardian technique tells no secrets.
    Mattingly has a secret in the storm.
We each have a secret hunger, but it is quelled by bread.
    We name-drop our own bed (and it breaks). Doing so says nothing.

What everyone in this room is doing while they sit quietly is a secret
   more beautiful to me than any speaker.

From a Photograph

how did I come to be autumnal,
a woman with unnew bones? how did
the secret of coffee escape me so long?
in my soft fantasy of wolves,
an excavation swallows the whole afternoon
until the search party retires to algebraic
weave, a lunatic sewing circle.
but for me, but if not for only me,
no stage fright, no Queen Mab,
no runs through the stockings of well-acquainted
visions. kites. it's so simple, this drab tea leaf,
this book of skeletons, knitted in two.

The Body of Elisabeth the Snake-Girl

I. Snake-arms

The girl with the shoulders of a snake
(while dancing) cannot recall the front teeth
of certain childhood playmates.
But did love the clack of Rummy-Q
tiles, loved to turn over the rack!
Always a sore loser even when delirious.
The snake-shouldered girl with the consonant lisp.
Takes off each thing as she acclimates
to her home each day each after-work arrival.
Front door: skating bonnet; armchair: glove; television:
velveteen slippers; archway: watchband; and so on.
The girl with the perpetual motion of a reptilian muscle
in her soft shoulders is most at home in her second skin.

II. Snake-bite

Why did Katy do this?
Katy was nasty; Katy bit the lipstick.
And chewed it. Katy is a bomb.
Katy is a firecracker in a red puff vest.
Katy made Elisabeth the girl who cried like a snake
cry. I tried so hard, said Elisabeth.
All I wanted was a salon of droll compadres
not smoking cigarettes not over cocktails
to read each other's artwork and say good good.
All I wanted was to give you three dollars.
Katy is not out of print but she is no longer accepting submissions.
There is a backlog of Katy, pink wax
flat and sticky pulp in her teeth.

III. Snake-charmer

The snake-girl sometimes talked like a cowboy,
sometimes an Egyptian. She always came late,
but the old women and the other, fleshier sorts
didn't care, because she (Elisabeth) brought candy
made from guava. "Darn," she would say, or
"best of luck!" but with a smoky vanilla accent.
Wore silver beads between her slit eyes.
The old women started a rumor her tongue was forked,
but it was all due to privilege. Even the Marxist
refugees recognized her flair, or flare-guns.
The silver spoon dislodged the moment
she cracked her own egg, cushioned in its woven basket.

IV. Snake-bird

Everyone likes a story about women braiding each other's hair.
"Let me jest scuff along yur scalp looking for rotten places,"
said the bad Snake Mama to Elisabeth.
She was raised with that sort of resilience,
but it culminated in her simply recommending psychotherapy
      to everyone she knew.
Or she'd say, "You should take yoga." Or
"Don't drink Coke—it's toxic sludge!"
Hair-pulling had made Elisabeth bossy
so that now in even the quiet moments
when she watched the corners of her mouth stretch in the
      bathroom mirror
under the stress of a glittered barrette,
something about her was not still.
There are wounds all over the neighborhood.

V. Snake-eyes

Elisabeth the snake-toed girl had a head cold.
Not one to complain, she removed the cancer with her incisors,
causing a riot later referred to by students as
"the last chance saloon." It was the illness

which kept away her many unknown companions.
Elisabeth knew the difference between visible.
She subdivided. [Please note: do not confuse
a worm for a snake. The one is mushy and inarticulate.]
One day when she will get better and not rheumy
a mess of scholarly patriots will aid her
with multiplication, incarnated as a board game
played up the path to a mansion haunted by divisibles of forty-two.

VI. Snake-doctor

(does she does she does she does she)
(only her hair-dresser knows for sure
who bejewels her each separate lock
of liquid metal pinned by a comb
fastened to resemble a dragonfly)
(in this Art Nouveau fashion Elisabeth
descends a staircase, or is a cousin
represented by a portrait hung in the drawing-
room like a haunting, a vain demon)
(for days after she's dyed her hair
to look like snakeskin, mottled or diamondback,
Elisabeth doesn't recognize the girl
with the iridescent _____ in café storefronts)
(something has been doctored, and the sweat
of ill health, of chemical change, is evident)

The Apple-Headed Doll

My nightmare house returns in the old hours,
its continuous stair and wax-work wing
exhibiting only one zombie by the mute piano:
the landlady who waits my rent with no tooth
and no vacancy in her black dress.
She is waiting again. I climb to her
and when the stair winds back I wind too.
Past the empty hallways. Up the velvet landings.
All the way to the marble ballroom. Her hollow eye.
Like the apple-headed doll, her skin shrunk back
to kiss against its barren core. And then she *is* a doll,
and my horror a dollhouse, each room
open at one end. And when I search
I find it, my tongue in the folds of her dark skirt.

Yesterday Yes

All the red bugs came back from their seaside vacation and sucked
    on the porous sidewalks.
The breeze was a little creepy, yes.
We ate late like they do in Spain.
But we're not in Spain, Cheryl said. That's the thing. This isn't Spain.
Yes. Yesterday we were inland, where there are bushes that people
    from Texas find frightening.
And we were coming to some kind of close.
A few of us may be packed up and shipped overseas.
We can only hope there won't be termites.
We hope the museum to which we are sent will be independently
    run and locally minded.
Yesterday we were of one local mind.
We weren't near a single body of water but yes we got sunburnt anyway.
And we didn't even lay out.
We were in the interior. It was outside, but an interior part of a not
    really coastal state.
We were walking, like they do in Spain.
We were suddenly fierce as bugs with shredding teeth.
We were counting on the night for a number of favors.
Each favor was red and completely American.

Metric: The Pleasures of the (keyhole)
after Ponge's The Pleasures of the Door

1. *They (female/male)*

the birds (male) do not reach the door
males do recognize not bliss or afternoons
held in their pockets: two sisters and one sculpture
moon is the grandfather of thefamily
above return, he is green, he is
taking the underground to the plaza (a meter) (a match)

2. *Us (inside)/two sisters*

ten bucks inside a woman, a keyhole
afternoon (bliss) embroidered
with twenty naked porcelain personages
moon of German stockings, all of one piece, a dune
my heart (a heart) rabid for the cell (which)
stalling in a marsh (or market) our retina
the eyes are severed and the heart enters you

3. *Mine all mine*

her toilet (rooms) are her new compartments
dune, my companion, is the retina of the heart
of wine of pockets
decisions and her brass clarity
it is inside of technique, blown glass, of wrestle
girlishness and a good lay (waylaid)
to the (limestone) graves of my last

What Else I Heard on the Radio

They will remove everything but your heart. Your heart they will rest in the husk of your dark body. All the other viscera goes in a clay pot and gets buried along beside you. But the heart they leave in its loose shell.

Isis is an Italian-American girl born in Niagara Falls who sings jazz. Not Jazz the girl but jazz, the lover kind, a cigar bar. Wide hips. Went to Catholic school. Makes a funny face like this: . Eats lots of red meat. I'm making her a bag to keep her tarot deck in. She once invited Christians inside from their barbeque of salt potatoes to browse around in her black hair. She's not prejudiced, but thinks the people who are claiming to be Moors are a bunch of slackers.

If your heart weighs more than her feather, you will go to paradise. If it weighs the same, and the scale hangs soft, you will be eaten by a big animal. You will be eaten by a crocodile, then a hippo, then a lion.

If you are dead for two thousand years, I don't want to wake you in some museum. That just isn't right. And so I leave the bodies intact, and only talk about their goldenness.

The Judge's Wife

(1)

There's a tower the lake calls Brother.
She whispers, *someone has lost a white dress*
in my eye that swims like nightfish.
Her brother answers, *stupid girl. That's the moon.*
The lake sleeps without pillows, on the wrong side,
the heart side.
She sings the song to herself:
Stupid moon. That's the girl.

(2)

A warlike house.

(3)

They salt their skin with ginger and then attack.
The females have thicker skin to survive the kisses.

A script: the monk, a charming politico, materializes to curse the
    black city.
I am carrying a rich woman's child.
One shoe has fallen and is lost.

There are many theaters. Shark theaters, starfish theaters,
theaters with the tops off.
Theaters with crowds waiting for night to reach their town,
pulling behind it lion cages and upside-down ladies pasted with
    red glitter.

(4)

I look back but don't see myself
in the lake. Don't see

the dress I lost. Don't see either brutal-
izing lover. Don't feel the sugar.

I notice I am emptier *with* you.

(5)

At what time of day did the judge's wife take her { } from the oven?
Head. Bun. Sheet cake. Bird.

At what time did the judge's wife call on her advisors?
The blue time. The tooth time. The current time.
The blue-green time.

At what hour did the judge's wife dissolve into my very own cave?
Sword. Bullet. Rope. Gas.

(6)

More violence and more nudity.

(7)

And so I never know which fountain we're at, or who invented the
fountain idea of a fountain in a park at all, or the idea of pedal boats.
Or the idea of swans.

(8)

The judge's wife makes a brief appearance
to throw a party she has coated in syrup
and gilded all the cakeboxes,
ordered fondue sets for everyone to take home as favors,
become what she is meant to becoming.

All her life she has wanted to avoid the bribe
when giving is her nature, a seahorse, a dragon
curled into its own spiny sweetness
at the sign of company. Treasure. Stranger.

(9)

If we made a baby, I would do all the carrying. You wouldn't even have to take one month.

(10)

The master removes a slice of cake from the slave.
It's what we don't understand
that pleases us, under a glass bowl.
Blue light, we're just a thin skin
for your surgical sectioning,
an orange for your silver knife,
a pear in a grove of golden balls and vine.
They have taken our keys to the end of the night.
We cannot drive, drunk as we are
on the judge's wife.
At the end of the night, our keys fall
off a cliff in wet embrace.

(11)

The tower has stolen another child, and all his children are white.
Bring me back my nightgown,
whimpers the moon, but she is squinting in the treedark.

The lake dreams she is a horrible girl who cannot tell the difference
    between a magician and a devil.

The lake dreams of years spent lost and naked in a marriage to the judge.

{she wakes} {still} {wet}

International Herald Tribune

Your newspaper is a two-star hotel:
~~facts~~ on strikes, vague about weather, clean sheets.
Not meant to match up so well.
What if, for instance, you went into the ~~priesthood~~
only to torture the local girls,
fully aware as you are of your own charms,
a bad version of a cockney accent, stagy?
What if you wore the collar & your hair
neat & short, to make them wild for you?
You justify it this way: a ~~temptation~~ which
keeps their minds on the pulpit.
In other stories, a business made a bundle last year
marketing "social communication."
Had a baby and took two days off.
You are headed to a resort for peace & quiet
with one thousand others dressed in the same irises,
canvas trousers. Your ~~imagination~~ at work.
Check out in the morning after saltines,
bridge lesson, make a clean break.
In the act of celibacy, what cannot be resolved
floats away in benday dots.

The Touchless Car Wash of Love

i gave you one promise & you handed it back whole
on the train ride home.
so i made up a song about the movie we saw.
& i used the wrong toilet again & again.
i asked you one question & it felled your chin.
now no one will sleep.
now there will be three possible car accidents with one broken
classroom in between.
bad timing.   the touchless car wash of love.
you work hard at the nothingness & i twice.
we admire wrists.   when we go to bed
we make enough room for a crib death.
blinkers   spray   & the rolled-up windows I adore.
safety (in numbers)   in the mess of it again & again.
i told you I'd write you this song
with neither of us knowing it'd be for you.

Counting Boys

I imagine the gods speak up: "we will

thread

the laces from some game in Michigan

into past & Xmas presents." The boys are so happy,

the twins. The everlasting. The skin of pigs.

Another suffragette speaks up: "the past is like an escalator,

its tight-lipped pout eternal into the floor."

"The future may in fact be

boys." Put them under a microscope

& count their dreams. Touchdown touchdown.

In the movies, long shadows or hawks, a predatory predate. Pregame.

Spilling into men, a wild wind, time,

my schizophrenia speaks up:

"lavender & yellow"

Pernod & water for me, thanks; beer

The Amityville Horror

Hey, Eloquence. Stardust. —— all about the common currency.
Without the gold —— just a girl who is equivalent of tending.
Soft-soap. Remember?

—— alone in the brass library. A bit of art: pagan, womanly.
—— plan on magic. Look it up in the card catalog. Under a
man's name. —— haunted? —— hope.

Don't eat the meat of animals —— swear to love. —— live by the
house of horrors, of swimming pools; by the synagogue (—— for
a short while belong. —— light modernist flame-buttons for
kaddish, the sorry dead. —— of toilet, the powder room, taffeta
dress.); by the cemetery.

One night —— walked until night was gone, a neighborhood of
very new houses. Was this the same silver street? —— didn't fear
—— soprano, or the abnormal smear of —— lynched sex, but
—— father drove —— home in a scotch glass and this was alien.
—— sat in —— stomach.

The second poem for ——. Maybe the third.

So suburban. At a loss for articles. Gendered out by sprinklers,
fine gram chemicals seeding & receding. All a sparkle. Ballerina.
Vanity.

Eat —— heart out. —— watch the movie about the toolshed,
about Jesus, about vomit. Things have gone too far, lack of sleep.
—— religion is a velvet cloak someone else will sew for —— to
wear to the rape fair. —— body-painted. Years of assholes.
Currency, remember gold? Celebrity?

—— tend to not believe in —— anymore until —— pass
—— house with the vacant camper and think of the Christmas

tree —— mother made, and ——, the woods of ——, pores, some Hawaiian perfume in a pot —— mentioned before, the plastic chain —— once wore taped to a black satin shirt, another girl wore a riding hat with a black veil, —— contacted the doors through a Ouija board, the times —— made fudge, undone now, drained.

happy holy

& say this here angels
angels in coral draped in lightning lull bugs
say internal internal internal s l o w combustion
say a star punched in tin
on the street where you lay
lay your sorrow head down
& it's gone inside all the red bugs are gone
say ginger root the nothing you hold in your hand
hold your hands like sifting sand
& hold it together but on the inside
in the kitchen with the red fire ants the beetles
& the small bugs that rhyme with star
say hallelujah come on get happy
a tin star punched in the parish hall
the bus parked outside
there is us
& there is a valley & there is the tight song the air forgot
there is the valley & the bugs loving their seeds
firehand starlight say the air rushes out
say the air does not rush at all but is
say is say is is is is is say a hole here
say hey here say hey to the star & bug parade
say learn here say burning head where you lay
& no more lonesome or ants of sorrow
& no more kitchen & no more tomorrow
& world without end here amen

News from the Front

With one father and one mother   a flood.
Transfer—underground laundromat to aid
the baby rebels. A war of bed sheets
that cannot stay dry.   I'm the son of sex.
Metro handjob   the floor of it   parents
above the linens. Let's not spread, she says,
any more of what you've wet. We all know
who is not there.   The bridge girl, so sorry,
a caution from the enemy   a spy
who is I   the infant maker of dry.

Tennessee

backwoods of New England, a new Dixie
fortnight ice, zero visibility,
we are the old South, slick invisible
passengers, a taste for miles, or four,
more gas, more patriarchs, everyone zoomed,
an atom out of the City where God
himself was born, chains on the tires, snow
in the treads, there's no roadmap or any
advice, Q: my savior, my mechanic, who
are you to tell me my fortune?, A: a white storm,

Gas Station Candy

We are moving out the horrors   mess hall
my brother a recluse star in a list
of stars, we can give more   futures, basket
for the passing   I am the boy who eats
wrappers, Pakistani postcards: I eat
for my mother   Our mentor   cellophane
is lost in yellowish sex   All my books
of organs spread in chocolate I'm not   lost
We are a great family, and mighty
Only a brief kiss/   suckers divide.

May Day

Me and my brother sleep in jennifer,
a gray mule, our sister (outer-space air).
A beautiful girl says, "yes, you had the
party" but she is a solstice of trash.
September next, the siblings will remove
to a city where love is made on curbs.
What will the neighbors think if I burrow
in the fur comfort of jennifer, in posters,
all over the subways? Velour
convertible, we celebrate garbage.

Katie Yates

a pocketbook: a purse of tubes: (rose cream)
in the stands of thin air: (omelets/pockets
of coyotes) grinning accountants write:
Katie Yates Katie Yates your sweet new book:
design for dreaming (the gold change of girls):
Katie Yates: a register of mountains:
what sends the angels driven into snow?:
is it grease for Katie?: a bottle of:
spray: of non-stick for Yates?: give her your card:
Katie Yates (caveshow), book girl, contact me

2° Gaslight

This Train

What comes more often than kisses to pollen is this train.
This train, the hands of god which are falsely.
The people who sleep with their socks on,
who slip their shoes off, into the hushtrip.
What comes more often than this punishment is.
And your father cannot hear any more; he drives.

This train, the hands of god which are falsely.
A cavity of pain which makes the hollow of sex.
Between a candle, all trains come for flight.
Electricity undoes like a later lover, a daughter.
And your father cannot hear anymore; he drives.
Plains contract: a groan along the belly of the road.

The people who sleep with their socks on,
day is over to them, adoring and abandoned.
The inside of her long body is a yellow flower.
Breathe here, in the small hole your life has made.
What comes more often than kisses to pollen is this train.
An egg, the day has frozen to the palms of your hands.

The Lady Vanishes

What if the landlady was a spy
& you & me were a broken pair of garage lights
a busted motion detector off & on all night & the landlady's son
really very nice like we didn't expect?
What if the magician were Italian
& the cardboard cutouts a whore
& the calf not a murdered or abducted spy at all?
What if you & me were neighborhood cats
& Latvia not the homewrecker we dreaded
& the scowling replacement in her tweedy hat was gone
as quickly as she came?
What if the moon was not full of berries
& the unborn next child still with his father?
What if your father was a straight shooter
& your mother taught music to the children?
What if the flower box was a red fish?
What if the hounds were quiet as hares
& you & me went tripping off to a sleeper compartment?
What if Europe was two feet long
& this was last May
& all was well?

The Lady from Shanghai

Being the second movie in as many days wherein
someone is "walked off" their overdose of sleeping
pills. And I remember what you wounded in my hand:
love. And I know the big fuck you. It's all captured
on film, tight as your father's basement boxing ring,
tight as ships. I walked under docks, under a fog of
that, the charcoal, and the untrust, spinning live wires
into the street that we made, aglow in the anarchy.
Was so safe, the poison, and the vomit. Which is not
to say we didn't watch it/enjoy the watching of it and
also the fucking out of anger, my body out of anger,
your fists out of this proves it, was real. And not just
the crutches (coming back to the movie) a million
times unsteady into the mirror. Hold the gun. We
point at each other, and the glass falls continually
away, shatter music. The "sharks who eat themselves
out," says Orson Welles, and I may not be now whole
or especially in the pool of what was us but. My
unhinged jaw is the ankle-trap, and I have found to
walk off in what I say. That's another language, out
of character, Chinese theater, and all the betrayals
finally belong. To me.

Hyponia

you have that pink-and-white shirt like a surly picnic
      that summons the fire ants from their larvae
you have that mouth that spells T O R N A D O
      propelling straw and Chryslers and everywhere
you have those eyes that are nighteyes:
      cicadas, unsung fog, a steam of sailors lost at sea

who made the popcorn? who made the movie? you?

you douse time and because of you we wear our wristwatches
      on the suicide side of our wrists

you have the ears that spilled blue cinders and caused Hawaii
you have the speech impediment which snaps off and on light bulbs
in neighbor yards all summer

when you die your talcum powder five deaths, we get lemonade
it's not fair so we celebrate Cyclothymia Day in your honor
      buy red and blue streamers, eat only flapjacks,
       listen to country singers at the wrong speed over public
      address systems on parade

you have the exact weight of three hundred and twenty-two sparrows
you have the lunchbox which grants us to catch fly balls
      when you replace the cap to your thermos
bless you o goddess of pop flies! and when it's not baseball season,
sanctify us with your everlasting balancing act, you who manufactures
      roadside carnivals
out of nothing, not even the smallest altar!

who made colored sugar? you? who made collateral?

we sit around at diners arguing your dogma over sunny-side-up
you sigh and our mailboxes fill with circulars

Foot and Mouth

The food was bad and so we got bad.
In fact, we got worse.

We got soggy and pink in the middle.
We carried our stomachs around like buckets.
We lied to customs and to each other.
We kept on eating.

We had just been to a continent
and now the continent was coming to us.
Through our meat. We became like a meat.
I looked at her and she had a meat neck,
and she said my own neck was marbled,
white rivers of fat where my vocabulary had been.

Little by little we grew accents.
We started to taste the hallowed mud.
It was like a farm had come down around us
and pinned us in place.
Even the red fence. Even the sky.

We bought a pasta maker.
We installed a calligraphy of tomato trellis in the yard.
We had all intentions to stop eating eggs.

It didn't matter.
One night she had the smallest horn.
By morning we were both mammals.

The Teeth of Betty Page

       removal. of flesh parcel
(these burning. lumps of coal) what can I. tell you?
an acre for an ✂ acre of eyes.

I will use. the opportunity of cancer
       to wear that bondage haircut

the girl cut apart by film ✂ the girl
cut apart by black panties ✂ the girl cut
into paper dolls bald. from her own eye-blades
(the way she sees herself on film)   a loop.

    ✂ look closer. it's a scalp. it's a scar.
it's the love of a good scalpel. it's all over.
I either wear it short or spend the vomiting hours
pulling the tangles from the bath.
I do love my breasts. they are so soft.
but I love my hair more. it's my rosetti.
my waterhouse. (I drown you out of) looker.
magnified.   messy stitches.   visible splice

The Girl

for George Saunders

No one knew that girl. She was nothing, a blue shawl.

Night came, blue night. It knew all the terrible choices. It covered the girl like a shawl.

In the morning, she was red. She was riding the red horse; no one chose to behave as if a catastrophe had come, but it had. They behaved as if breakfast was breakfast and not actually a terrible morning.

They covered their mouths with shawls. In a fit of jealousy, they chose a new horse, a blue horse. They rode to town, where night was not actually night—it was a vest pocket for girls, a sullen catastrophe.

They rode back to the kitchen where the girl was covering her smile.

Where was the night, its breakfast? Why did it not behave? She knew; they knew. No one chose to know. If a catastrophe actually happened, there would be jealousy coming out of the oven like red milk, the milk of sullen horses.

What a catastrophe! Nothing all over, blue shawls, oven mornings. The girl was in a fit, fit of smiles. What was in her pocket? What terrible jealousy was in her mouth?

Come, she said. Come choose the terrible choice.

Interview by the Name of Hydrant

don't wake the baby but
My man doesn't come around here anymore.
He's gone and went. He's gone and gone.
And the sink's so full of limbs the ants are going nutty.
I put the steaks and milk out on the curb, the full bucket.
I put up a shelf and lined it with wax.
It's like a crib death around here. Like a low song.
Nothing lonesome, mind you, but sort of snaky.
There's a long moan that's a part of it, and a hiss,
of insects coming aboard. We're all in this together.
Get out the violins.
And I'll tell you another thing.
About the countertops? They are like pure gratitude.
I don't know what that means, but I know it.
Hey, if you can think of a craft project that requires eight or so
discarded black vinyl sleeves for the Pill,
let me know. I'm thinking something like an advent calendar,
only with nights for where the bad parts come in.

The Secret History of Chocolate

The magician's assistant is a historian. She gives a radio interview. She speaks warmly, says to the callers, "what a profoundly interesting question." They are grateful. They haven't read the book yet, but they will, they say. They won't.

Hat Trick: Lucy got pretty sad about living in a country where the government can say no to the name you give a child, even though she had no child. She got sad about having no child, especially no girl child named Zenobia. So Lucy put on a kind of hard safari hat and discovered cacao, a bush, a bean, a flower, two kinds of crazy-making powder, and it cheered her up a bit.

To be a magician's assistant, you must first believe in the real as a Fact in itself. Without the real, there is no awe at its breakage. Lucy was trained in basic chemistry and liked large dogs. She was as real as they come.

The assistant is applying glitter. There was a time when she wanted to embody the word "Pixie." Something about an x in the middle, a very short haircut requiring no brush. Every girl, most girls, some girls go through this pixie stage, which often also incorporates: see-through unicorn window decals, hologram pencils, and the making of, yes, fudge. You see.

Embalming is a process involving replaced fluids. To make the dead appear napping, a face is painted. Special make-up, Lucy assumes. Not Wet n' Wild.

"There is something magical about this realism," the audience exclaims, delighted, somewhat dopey on little paper cups of swirled ice cream served with tongue depressor spoons glued to the lids. "It's the chocolate," Lucy says flatly, removing the knife from between her teeth. "I invented it to make you happy."

To perform my next trick, I will require a tin of herbal lip balm in a castor oil base, a push pin, some hydrogen chloride, and one simple Kleenex. May I have some assistance from the audience, please?

Lucy makes a very sad grown-up girl. She moves from one continent to the next, adjusting her leotard. In Dallas, she misses and the rabbit turns out a disturbingly dark shade of red. It doesn't matter, she notices. The whole crowd is listening to their own collective heartbeat, cocainized on the Milk Duds.

"So that's how I invented chocolate," says the magician's assistant, and smiles at the host, which nobody can see, but they can hear the smile. "When I'm dead they'll remember me for it." "Thank you," says the host, "for blocks to chop, for chips, for sauce, for hard shell, for fondue, for squares, for Mexican, for hot, for white, for dark, for unsweetened." "It was nothing," says Lucy. "I was sad and I was on a lost continent with no children and I needed something to do in between acts, in between being reconnected with my torso or attaining visibility." "Well, thank you again for it," says the host. "You're all such idiots," says Lucy.

The Libertine

She dreams she buys a red sports car
with a six thousand dollar check she can't cover
returns it to the lot three days later.
Black-haired men, a terrible mistake:
hot vinyl against her thighs; the round, sour eyes; full day's shade
    of beard.
She beats her pillow
screams I'm not kidding! You need to take it back!
The waking world is a swollen relief.

Her blackest stockings are open at the heels.
The holes stutter up her ankles.
She darns nylon thread with nylon thread, a lost art.

She marches a path to the sink and its black tar soap.
She washes her hands so often her skin peels off in little voids,
    pearly scars.

She avoids the turn of the century
fastens herself in the black beaver coats and lace-up boots of the last.
The shadow of a sundial, of a microwave carousel, hides half her face.

To My Beaux-Artsy Bedfellow

Here you come, a thrush
picked clean between your teeth,
fine white bone,
the crown of a little neck the size of a knuckle.
What is the meaning of this?

Are you the one loosening the appliances from their jacks?
Who scurried sidelong across the concrete walls
of my laundry room on an odd number of legs?
I've been looking for you.
Feverish, in the ditch between dream & awake,
you make sense, a steaming pile of it.
We dine, me & your shadow.

Are you male or just malnourished?
The shell we occupy beats its mothwings like an ailing heart.
The internal is an untended hearth, ash everywhere.
Let's wrestle in the pillows. Let's make a fort
with flashlights underneath. So ornate, no resolve,
but at least a flush, a full house, a flush.

Tour of —— Morning Farms

The round   (hours)   tucked in each   iron   bell
        worn by goats   (wormed, hoofed):
a lie & a lust.   Nightmare knockings
            of shoehorn testicles against the clapboard door,
neighbor   (trampy)   horse, shaking her head no no no.
The boys   (white-haired, hockey)   are allergic
    to that which   is not shit,   not that spray of weed,
                not rubber boots upturned all through the loft,
        lost spaniels splaying their tongues.
Two trays of soap (on the counter):   olive   rosemary
                various saps & seeds,   starved marble.
The tight face the sun makes.   We pull out
            from the hormones of fresh cheese,   from solar panels
grinding dimmer & dimmer roots,
 the cellar
& its jars of Mason,   whatever,   fraternal;
                (disorder this skinned life carries)
towards the edge of organic,   plunge into
            a brisk & clear shot of filament,   process,   spasm.

Berlin Series
for E.

I. Basement

If you don't know boys, you can't follow them. It has always been
this way. When I was smaller, boys were larger. They have circles
for heads, and in the cartoons, everything is backwards and made
from dots. In dreams, boys pray or they make trouble. It has
always been this way. This is a poem about a war.

II. Dizzy

The music of the Ancient Egyptians was something like be-bop,
only more orange. The music of New Jersey is asphalt and brothers.
In the fields there is a horror that takes place. I ran from it,
knowing that the mouth of something which can't speak is not
hardly a mouth at all. Music is in the organs. By this I mean the
heart and also the belly. Is music a criminal? I think that children
know this answer.

III. Push

Vision is a guess made by the power of subtraction.
This is obviously about a person alone.

IV. Casual

And here we again return to music and to felony.
Always where there is a radio there is the desire for company,
and the desire for relaxation, and also the desire, perhaps, for touch.
When I was a child I had many positions, and some of them
involved leaning and some made me expose my body. In this way I
made friends.

V. This

If you live in a city your whole life, you naturally end up wanting air. It is a natural thing. The children of cities, especially, let's say, the boys of smaller cities near the places they manufacture newspaper, want air and they think they want trees. But they don't really want the trees. *Ce n'est pas naturel.* Neither is love.

VI. This

We make marks, and in this way we are like the species of fish who leave their ink when they are frightened. Artists are very much like terror, terrified fish. At least, that's the medical side of it. You could say I got this piece of advice from my brother, but it is not related completely.

VII. Died

We do not trust ourselves. The chain of being is passed from father to son. For me it was passed in a field with a spray can. It is all in toys, the memory, and this shows how I am not ready to give up the toy. This shows how all memory is false. As you can see, this is about a lost dog.

Green Lakes

Lou Reed Lou Reed save them
who don't want to go down in shallow water
that don't want to drown in the little black lake
Lou Reed you know what these Syracuse winters are like
everyone becoming their cat and on top of that
the pipes freeze
don't let them choke the pipes
don't show them how to fellate for exhaust
Lou Reed come on step off the stage
they need the clamorous party
they are a lot like a lake with all the roots
showing bones of lowness there
nothing sky nothing moon nothing holes
and you know where all the rotten holes are
so be kind come alive
accept your diploma and your drinking mouth
the whites of your eyes in their little black house
they're going on a little vacation Lou Reed
a little Delmore Schwartz vacation into the gas tubs
and the bottom is coming up to meet them
and the little black teeth are singing a song
stop them stop them give them a sun

Nostalgia, Cheryl, is the Best Heroin

The house knows this and the kitchen knows this.

The shingles tastes of lovers, and the little bedroom is the girl whose lover has bruised her into what he thinks he knows he wants.

He thinks. He knows. He wants. A dark little house. The afghan of tenderness.

In front of the bruise, the townspeople have gathered for the nod-out into plush plush love, so easy and out. The cabinet wants more. This community of beating. This neighborhood of oblivion. The cabinet has less and wants more.

This is a terrible story, Cheryl. It is an instructional essay for a sweet beating. It is an open letter to linen closets everywhere.

Where does the girl keep her lust for the past hidden, in case the punishers come?

The house pushes for its needs. He needs.

The dishtowels, Cheryl, they are all so limp, so exhausted from the avoidance of sex. The oven is white with love. The couch is falling in under the weight of personal memory: too tight, too wired.

An electric horse, this little house addiction.

The mouth of the garage is dry and has no bicycles.

The lover is beat and the lover is over.

Bend over, tender dream. And ready for the smack. The window-frames are abused of their hunger. And he forgets. And the house keeps on.

Myth of Moths

can you tell a ghost story can I
our mouths come apart in our hands
we touch surfaces counters chipped rapture
back porch can hear me scream
out of tenderness here is the bruise
here is the moment I lay down for you
I was wet I wept we talked about cider
after the film orange moths cling to our
home can you tell a story the thing
which returns again and again to the site
of its own thingness its thrashing its crime
yank back the curtain to see scrubbed raw
sloshing in the bottom of the well
freshly dug my gap some skin from
which I extract blades the sudden hands
white in the pitch-dark a thousand wings

Grunting Calliope

for Kirsten Kaschock

toys don't sleep. in the bedrooms of sickly children, they keep a
restless vigil. some say "when you close your eyes, they move, or
leave the room" but it is in fact all the time that they do this. they
revolt all the time.

toys don't sleep—the chinaman breaks—
they wrap up on the tarmac—
teacups + saucers—a sugared carnival—vodka girl—nervous
collapse dreamer—or boy with haircut—fish hands—

are you drunk yet? have we filled your mouth with perfumed oil,
made you flaccid? did you brag about the worse kids to someone
who could care less?

did you brag about what is—puppeteer—suspended—beautiful—
post office—returns the syringe
to—streptococcal sender—hunting
+ fishing—a flying—party dress—fish—sunrise—topsy—
water bearer of—hash—little tire-dout slut bad—tremble—can—

spun out. a brother of no one cracked up the car. crashed into
the barrier. it was a holiday. his death was a national holiday, but
he recovered and we went back to school. we slid our trays down
the conveyor for service, a meatloaf shaped like a rabbit.

windmill—tremolo—service tray service—glassware—
entrance—tighten cuckoo—ballast—
a pair of arranged marriages—cee a gram—very blunt scissors—of—

the two nod out with their wrists so delicate. when you pass them,
you think "how could." It's a very stupid question. as if you
yourself never wanted to be unlike your own mother.

white laundry machine powder—shake it
off—dogtag leashed—countrified judo—westward
—buttonholed—widow's peak—clockwork—asking for
the maid—aflutter—antimatter cranium—gorilla—

that's really rude. we look at each other's eyewhites during the
performance to make sure no one is sleepy or coughing or looking
for snacks. we sleep and in the sleep we are at a birthday party, it is
our turn to ride the pony.

smack fresh can:—we ride the pony—
wear—fun to be a martini—the little cone-
like hat what is—chamber of locusts—
bad check—in particular—a particle

what about it?

The Giant

The giant is a girl.
How can I connect this to a cream-and-brown bicycle?
In a childhood mishap, the giant is a girl without a helmet.
How can I relate this to my sister?
The giant is a lonely girl. A too-thin girl.
How can this be part of my Treatment?
The giant, a girl, accepts Divine Love as her Light.
How can I cross this over the border into Canada?
The giant is a girl with a taste for sugar.
How can this meet the feeling in my legs?
The giant is a girl who often fails to notice flowers.
How can this be turned into a novel?
At night, the giant is a girl writing letters.
How can this imitate hand-letterpress?
Stop. The giant weeps.
How can I take this into the living room?
She hangs an unfinished pastel drawing on her wall, close to the
    ceiling, shoulder-height.
How can I get you to kiss the back of my neck now?
The giant eats a bowl of ice cream. Her stomach hurts.

Corn Palace/Moon Palace

The moon palace is a —phile of everything you're selling.
Rain down on me, she says. *I'm just your speed.*
Her rooms are translucent, her eyes are zombied,
but she rolls on stockings that glint at the knee.
Come on, she says. *My legs are the tastiest river.*

In the corn palace, a movie blinks envy envy envy on every frame,
whimpering, *That's my lover you're threading, Moon.*
Give her back to me. A palace made of stacks. History.
Place of no names but Soon.
A brush of grain across the empty dancehalls.

This is Missouri. Or this is Acapulco.
This might be the soundtrack to an underwater volcano.
This could be the summer everyone you know went into remission
and you were left alone with your Schedule C,
on which you wrote *Deduct expense of paying*
to hear that swing band play their bones out with M.
Deduct thirty cents a mile to get to the devil's picnic, where Corn lay in wait.
Deduct one half of every moment I spent separating
moonlight from popcorn, stone from stalk, silver from gold,
those two ladies fighting over you like you were a Waterlily
and they were the last two museums on earth.

Alter (Mexican Retablos)

Dear ~~Gary Nausea~~ Gary,

You know. I am that cannibal.

She is de Sade   but I dreamt the red moon
a borderlands   My coat is full of roses
the frostbite of my sex   which she currently
owns   or barter   She is besotted

Christ is raving   He gave her   "completely twisted up"

A tin church   correspondent   The Madonna
of paper towels (shit shit shit)
                              Let's burn
something for the portrait of two weeping
saints   Let me wish you health   Musicale
Hyper-musicale
                To prevent hunger let me
presuppose I will not stop myself though my particular pathology
      leads to both fragmentation and mania

Saint Our Lady for removing ill
Saint Christ of bread

With amaranth   saliva of tin   of
rocks   "no particular patronage"   but
the turquoise I once knew in Portugal is in fact present
                And the Eye of God
who follows me like a sweet roller-skate

no   not this
I want a poem for my lover

Saint Lugrada of no background
Saint Gansalvus of bridges
Saint Francis of arson

Saint Rosalia of engagement
Saint Hermanita of proscenium
Saint Camilo of podiatry
Saint Sorrow of seven
Saint Leonard of the martyr's handwriting
Saint Joseph of foster and decks/patios
Saint Child of miracle donkeys and aortas

The hand of the eye of god   her red
blood the lambs spit back

LA. Ma. No. Po. D^e Ro. Sa

Saint Isidor of lush
Saint Pity of that peeking moon

A man in overalls lights the queen
"Having been greatly altered in the head," I
make a portrait that exists in photographs   in dreams of men
    A miracle

Saint Refuge
Saint Juan of "death trance"
Saint Rita of absolute terror
Unknown Saint with three nails
Saint Anthony of objects

A thousand plastic babies for your charms   I wish
you nothing if not distance   a pool of white
paint where she left off   the side of hips

Is it not terrible what I palm a confidence artist in the wine a confidence
    lacking a confidence?
This secret   slashed from
my chest   the lodged thorn   we disagree
on the famine   with tinctures then I
remove the eye which triangular watches
        in punched altar,
        Arielle

The Third Man

Dear passport. Dear orphan-with-ball.
Dear balloon man. Dear sewer.
When we die, we carry ourselves across our own streets.
We have lost the address.
Mortality is the business of the window-washer,
the men with long sticks (for getting) the job done.
Dear shadow.
We keep our hands in the pockets of our trench coats,
the play—a little shovel of dirt.
A little violin music for the woman eating soup.
Dear dilution.
Europe is down around the mouth,
and a barbershop quartet of policemen in costume
follow the cats to the shoes of their lovers,
the gum of night.
Dear posies. Dear landlady. Dear scandal.
We open the box to show you our fingers.
We open the streets to show you our spine.

Address Slightly Wrong

They had an electronic baby and named it a mixture of their two names run together like a lake. A lake name. From the baby they sent out invitations: "be a baby!" Be my baby. They bought it a baby bathrobe to hide it like a tiny prune. They took out their earrings and put them on the bedside table before making love so nothing would get caught. They couldn't have a baby at all, so they had stomach aches. They had phone calls, and folk songs about trucking. They had palms which read "much weekend travel." They drank a cup of tea. They thought they knew themselves. They were born in October. They replaced someone born in October. A little something scurried in the corner. Of their eye. Scurried. They were hollow. They had their tooth fixed.

An agent came out of a dark shack and told them the story of their twinhood. It was a bad story with lots of parts about their birthday, a day of "finite detail." It was a combination of stories about the way love and its complications make regular people do the strange things regular people all do. The explanation only made them lonelier. When one of them left, the other one put nails in the recipe box. When the other one left, the first one tasted dust. Their father-in-law barked like a dog because he wasn't either father. The government sent them a form: "choose a new name, one that belongs to no one, and tell us what color you are." They were yellow. They chose the name Day.

Sentences for Babycat

You hung the moon, sugarbean.

There was a pink and a pink in the breakfast of every turtle,
a tiny pea, and you did it.

You made the campgrounds all Crystal Gale.

You are the jewel of the eye that is Swimmy.

There was a butter swirled into caramel.

When I am warmest I am made.

Sweetest slice, be only what you already are:
not a bank torn from beaches,
not a good mitten with string,
but the cat of your spine,
rubbing head, all shining teeth.

Given

—— has become a Blowdryer

which is to say   a winding of cat tongues around a spool

causing heartbreak   in all the gaskets   (*I don't in the least*)

if —— were only   in the days of jelly roll and apron

if —— were only   the beautiful slave trade

(*the little round ways —— loves you*)

no guesses for the identity   of the jailer here

excuse, excuse: diffuse   a contraption for complexity

when first encountering the Look of love

a wooden door   to a sort of Breton village

(*sugar   lemons   cream of lemons*)

stream for the brain

to paraphrase: white   dead eyes of the mister

it's a kind of frown a name

kind of a vaginal/Duchampy frown

tenderest slit   the sound of an envelope

the question is who gets posted

—— is without fever   without "eyes"

or the terrible truth is   well   terrible

fictive as that wiring   which controls

cellular material   spread

in the afterlife —— is so accommodating   a gift

of gaslight   murdered by air

Sea Legs

sea legs
come back to me
so they float across the ocean
unbent at the knee
in little white socks
whispering *dolce, dolce*
& looking like girls
flesh
only shorter
sea legs
I've been so blue without you
just this wind in my ear
& this knife at my throat
thighs
that were mine
& widowed me to the pavement
a peak
at my gray gate
empty pail
but now for berry season
or a scale of convex sequins
sea legs
come floating back to me

Notes & Acknowledgments

Some of these poems previously appeared (sometimes in slightly different versions) in the following publications: *3rd Bed, American Letters & Commentary, Bird Dog, Can We Have Our Ball Back?, Chase Park, Conduit, Crayon, Fence, The Hat, Hunger, Insurance, ixnay, LIT, Mirage #4/Period(ical), Outlet, Pleiades, Prosodia, Quarter After Eight, Slope, untitled, Verse* and *Volt.* My deepest thanks to the editors.

The poems in (caveshow) were written from dream material by David Kirschenbaum using "rules" he devised. The poems previously appeared in the chapbook *Light Sleepers* (Green Cherries, 2000). Thanks to David and to Aaron Kiely, whose reading series in Cambridge was the impetus.

"The Lady from Shanghai," "The Third Man," and "Pathos" appeared under the title *Cotton Wells: Three Film Poems,* as OASiA Broadside no. 70(g) by Stephen Ellis of Oasis Press for the Third Annual Boston Poetry Conference.

A grant from the Constance Saltonstall Foundation for the Arts gave me time and encouragement to work on this book. I am very grateful.

More gratitude, and much love, to my family. The same to Melissa Anderson, Maile Chapman, Elizabeth Treadwell Jackson, Kirsten Kaschock, Linda Russo, Cheryl Strayed and Rachel Zucker, all brilliant women writers and thinkers, and to Beth Anderson for requiring me to put this manuscript together in the first place. Thanks to the Syracuse University MFA program. Special thanks to my teachers, especially Lyn Lifshin and Michael Burkard. And to Rob Morris, for everything.

The book's title and two of the section subtitles are taken from Marcel Duchamp's final work, *Etant donnés: 1° la chute d'eau, 2° le gaz d'eclairage,* which resides in the Philadelphia Museum of Art.

Arielle Greenberg was born on October 24, 1972 in Columbus, Ohio. She subsequently lived all over New York State—in Niskayuna, Schenectady, Binghamton, Westchester, NYC (Astoria and Long Island City, Queens), and Syracuse—and in Haifa, Israel (from 1987 to 1988). She was educated at Hebrew day school, public high school, SUNY/Purchase College and Syracuse University. In the early 90s, she was the publisher of *William Wants a Doll*, a pop culture zine; her essays and reviews on literature and art currently appear in *Rain Taxi*, the *Electronic Poetry Review*, *Women's Studies* and other journals. She is the recipient of a Saltonstall Individual Artist's Grant and a MacDowell Colony fellowship and serves on the editorial board of *How2: an Online Journal of Innovative Women's Poetics*. Since 2001, she has lived just outside Boston.